50 games for active toddlers

Quick everyday hints and tips to keep toddlers
active, healthy and occupied

NICOLA COOPER-ABBS

*Discover more books and ebooks of interest to you and find out about the range
of work we do at the forefront of health, fitness and wellbeing.*

www.ymcaed.org.uk

Published by Central YMCA Trading Ltd (trading as YMCAed).
Registered Company No. 3667206.

Central YMCA is the world's founding YMCA. Established in 1844 in Central London, it was the first YMCA to open its doors and, in so doing, launched a movement that has now grown to become the world's biggest youth organisation. Today, Central YMCA is the UK's leading health, fitness and wellbeing charity, committed to helping people from all walks of life – and particularly the young and those with a specific need – to live happier, healthier and more fulfilled lives.

ISBN: 1492985511
ISBN-13: 978-1492985518

This book is presented solely for educational and entertainment purposes. The author and publisher are not offering it as legal, medical, or other professional services advice. While best efforts have been used in preparing this book, the author and publisher make no representations or warranties of any kind and assume no liabilities of any kind with respect to the accuracy or completeness of the contents and specifically disclaim any implied warranties of merchantability or fitness of use for a particular purpose. Neither the publisher nor the individual author(s) shall be liable for any physical, psychological, emotional, financial, or commercial damages, including, but not limited to, special, incidental, consequential or other damages, resulting from the information or programs contained herein. Every person is different and the information, advice and programs contained herein may not be suitable for your situation. Exercise is not without its risks and, as such, we would strongly advise that you consult with your healthcare professional before beginning any programme of exercise, especially if you have, or suspect you may have, any injuries or illnesses, are currently pregnant or have recently given birth. The advice, information and guidance given in Central YMCA Guides are in no way intended as a substitute for medical consultation. As with any form of exercise, you should stop immediately if you feel faint, dizzy or have physical discomfort or pain or any other contra indication, and consult a physician.

CONTENTS

ABOUT THE AUTHOR

My name is Nicola Cooper-Abbs and I was born in a small town in the north of England in the 1970s. I'm fairly sure I came out clutching a pencil and pen and asking where the nearest library was. Predictably, I grew up to be writer, studying journalism at the University of Central Lancashire and then moving over to the world of marketing and PR. I spent a couple of years working in an agency, had a quick pit stop in New Zealand and taught English in the exotic location of Salford, England. Ten years ago I set up as a freelance writer and marketer.

I now spend my time writing about a variety of parenting topics combined with my role as Marketing Director of MumPanel, a specialist insight consultancy. But my most important job is being mum to my two chatty, hilarious and truly wonderful girls.

INTRODUCTION

I'm a mum to two girls, aged six and three, and so I've spent much of the last six years coming up with new and imaginative ways to keep them occupied. My girls are an energetic pair who love nothing better than being outside but when you live in a country where it rains (a lot) you have to get creative when it comes to keeping them active. My ideas have come from my own imagination, talking to other parents, taking them to groups, resources from preschool and daycare and calling on my own childhood.

But there were days when I was stumped – we'd played all our favorite games and they were still full of beans. I'd usually end up taking to the internet to come up with something new to do. But what I could have done with was a quick guide, something I could just flick through when I needed some inspiration. And that is how this book was born. I hope it will act as a handy resource that you call on time and time again to find new ways to play with your toddler and spark your own imagination.

HOW TO USE THIS BOOK

This book is designed for mothers and fathers, grandparents and carers who need ideas to keep little toddler bodies occupied. Maybe you'd love to be more active with your toddler but can't come up with ideas, or you just need inspiration for cold, wet days when you are stuck inside with a hyper 2 year old. This isn't a heavy duty guide laden with expert opinions; it's a simple guide with everyday hints and tips. It's packed with lots of ideas from my own experience, from parents and grandparents at daycare and the school gate. We've also called on the imagination of hundreds of parents from specialist mother-marketing and insight consultancy, MumPanel. The idea is you have an accessible book that you can dip in and out of when you need inspiration. It covers indoor and outdoor play and includes ideas that are free or that cost very little.

The book is broken down into five chapters, from looking at why being active is important in Chapter 1 to what games you can play in the house and how to create a good play environment in Chapter 2. Chapter 3 looks at getting out and about – from playing in parks to what to do at the beach. In Chapter 4 we'll explore different clubs and organizations that offer play opportunities and round up in Chapter 5 by looking at how long-standing ideas of active play can work alongside a world packed full of technology. At the start of each chapter are some quick game ideas when you need an instant way to keep the kids occupied. In each chapter you'll find lots of ideas for active and healthy games. Let's get playing!

Important safety notice

Toddlers and young children should always be supervised by an adult when playing. Please check all play equipment regularly to ensure it is safe.

1

ACTIVE AND HEALTHY GAMES TO PLAY WITH YOUR TODDLER

PLAY TRENDS FOR THIS YEAR: Kids play outside less than their parents did – the JCB Fresh Air Campaign research showed that children played outside for 2 hours during the 1970s and 1980s and that has now dropped to just an hour a day.

QUICK GAME IDEAS:

- Kick a ball – try rugby balls or lightweight beach balls
- Play catch – use different weights and sizes of balls
- Egg and spoon races – hard-boiled eggs work best!
- Trampolining – at home or in a local leisure center
- Tickle chase – see if they can escape before the tickle monster catches them
- How many laps – give your child a time (say, one minute) and see how many laps of the kitchen/garden/park he or she can do
- Make a den – use blankets, beds and sofas inside, and sticks, leaves and old sheets in the garden or woods
- Play in the sandpit – get them digging in the sand, building castles and looking for buried treasure
- Swings and slides – find a local park and have some fun on swings, slides, climbing frames and roundabouts; a great way for toddlers to build confidence

- Bat and ball games – start with a plastic bat and lightweight ball; a good family sport

When I asked parents for their ideas to include in this book, the one thing I heard time and time again was that our kids don't play outside as much as we older generations used to. Whether that's down to wanting to protect our kids, or televisions and technology taking over, parents still want their children to be active and healthy. In the MumPanel survey, "Playing Games with your Toddler," 67% of parents said they really wanted their children to be active and healthy. But sometimes things get in the way of being active and healthy with our kids – from work to the weather, having enough money or space at home or our own lack of energy. When this happens we need a reason to get off our behinds and make the time and space to play with our kids (or find things that promote independent play).

SO WHY DO CHILDREN NEED TO BE ACTIVE?

- It promotes healthy growth and helps them hit developmental milestones (play helps develop a number of skills including gross and fine motor skills and hand–eye coordination).
- It improves balance and flexibility.
- It helps them grow a strong body and bones and improves posture.
- It helps to maintain a healthy heart and good weight.
- It gives them the chance to interact with other people, make friends and improve their self-esteem.
- It gives your child a way to relax.

The general recommendation is that children have at least 60 minutes of physical activity a day which should include a mixture of moderate and vigorous aerobic activity (for example walking to school and running) and muscle and bone strengthening activity (for example climbing trees and skipping rope). This hour of activity doesn't have to happen all at once but it's a good idea to find ways to encourage active time that's away from screens.

PLAY: WHAT TO THINK ABOUT

1. Starting early
It's never too early to start being active with your children. Even before they are up and walking you can encourage their development and lay down good habits by finding healthy ways to interact with your child.

Idea: *"I often move around the room and move her toys to encourage her to move about* *and crawl to get what she wants, rather than handing everything to her."* **Gillian, mother to Isabelle, 9 months**

2. Where to find ideas

When we asked parents where they got their ideas from, 79% said they came from what they played when they were little, 75% from their own imagination, 68% from friends and 49% from the internet.

You could also check out parenting books, the local library, preschool and daycare for their resources, toddler groups and blogs.

Idea: *Use your own imagination – let the child in you free. When was the last time you ran across the park? How about a shoulder ride? Or sitting your toddler on your knee and playing ride the horsey (hold their hands and bounce them up and down while shouting, "Ride the horsey, neighhhhh!"). Don't be embarrassed, just let go and have fun!*

3. Involving family members and friends

Play doesn't have to involve you; it's good to foster independence in your child and find ways to encourage interaction with other people who bring their own ideas and creativity. Ask family members what games they remember playing as a child (maybe hopscotch or pick-up sticks) and ask them to teach that game to your child.

Idea: *"I also let her play with aunts and uncles as well as my younger friends and they have even more fun ideas."* **Zuzanna, mother to Julia, 10 months**

4. Play dates

Children who aren't keen to play or be active can be encouraged to take part by the enthusiasm of other children. Set up play dates with friends – anything from some planned activities at home to throwing a tennis ball in the park.

Idea: *Invite friends over and have some activities planned. How about drawing circles with chalk outside or seeing who can do the most jumps in a minute?*

5. Planning

One thing that catches us out when it comes to play with our kids is our lack of time and energy. It can be a struggle to come up with ideas when you are tired or you come up with an idea only to find you are missing something you need to play the game. So how about starting a games kit with a notebook (this book would be a good start to which you can add your own ideas) jam packed with games and activities that you can turn to when you lack inspiration.

Idea: *Lead the way by showing your toddler that you are an active and healthy family. Find time to walk to school or daycare rather than going in the car. Go for a walk or bike ride in the evening. Give them jobs around the house that keep them active (carrying small piles of washing, putting cups and plates away).*

6. Getting the right equipment

As part of your games kit, it's worth investing in a few basics – a skipping rope, a light larger ball, a smaller ball (tennis ball), a beanbag, plastic bats, hula hoop, cones, a Frisbee. If you can afford them, water or sand pits are very versatile. This gives you some immediate play options and the basis of a variety of games.

Idea: *Invest in a waterproof play mat, such as a Tuff Spot. These large plastic trays are brilliant for indoor and outdoor messy play. You can sometimes pick them up secondhand on websites such as eBay.*

7. Learning new skills

You already know being active helps your child's development, but it can also be a great way to learn new skills. How about teaming up with friends and having weekly bike or scooter rides? You can start with babies or toddlers in a seat on your bikes and progress to their own trike, scooter or bike. Don't forget a cycle helmet and pads.

Idea: *Crazy Golf. Set up a golf course using bits you find around your house (boxes, tubes from kitchen paper, blocks). Give your toddler a golf stick (long cardboard tube, the inside of wrapping paper works well) and a ball (tennis balls) and then show your toddler how to move the ball around the obstacles.*

8. Teaching cooperation and sharing

One issue parents told us they have when it comes to active play is finding something that will occupy a toddler and their older siblings (or friends). It's worth having a few games that foster teamwork and appeal to different age groups – parents told us that favorites are hide and seek, obstacle courses where they have to work together to get across, and team games suitable for all ages, such as football. Play games that involve sharing (passing the ball games, relay races – great fun if you play with teddy bears). Older siblings are also a top resource for game ideas so it's worth asking them what they think would work for your toddler.

Idea: *Does your toddler drive you crazy following you around all day? Why not turn it into a game! Teach your toddler to follow the leader and you can have fun while getting jobs done.*

9. Something different every day

If you have your child at home with you all day, every day, then it's worth taking some time to structure games and activities. Consider focusing on a different activity for each day – so Monday is body day, Tuesday is day out activity (park, beach), Wednesday is music and dance day, and so on.

Idea: *Make Monday body day. Explore with your toddler all the different ways your body moves. Can they jump like a jack in the box? Can they bend backwards? How many directions do their legs move in? How high can they reach their arms?*

10. Let them run free

As horrifying as letting a toddler run free sounds, we're suggesting you actively encourage it (in a safe way). That means think about the basics – restricting their time in front of the television, or sitting in highchairs, car seats, or being carried. Work on them walking and getting active. It does mean you'll probably need an extra set of eyes in the back of your head but it's worth it to see your child making developmental leaps and being as healthy as possible.

Idea: *Make a safe play area in your home, free of obstructions, with a gate if needed, where they can play happily and independently for a short while so you can shower, for example. You can still keep them active during this time by scattering toys that they have to find.*

2

PLAYING IN

QUICK GAME IDEAS:

- Football/soccer – there are lots of toddler-level classes or you can just kick a ball around in your local park or garden
- Row your boat – a fun way to get physical while singing. Sit opposite your child on the floor, take their hands and pull and push gently while singing "row, row, row your boat, gently down the stream" so that you are helping to stretch their whole body. Try speeding up or slowing down the song and actions
- Building towers – great for hand–eye coordination and fine motor skills. Use building blocks, or for larger outdoor towers use cardboard boxes or Tupperware
- Swimming – if you start early, most children love being in the water and it's a good way to get exercise for both you and your child
- Tag – the simplest of all chase games. One person is it and chases everyone else until they tag another person, who becomes it and the game continues!
- Croquet – you don't have to have the whole set, you can start with just a long cardboard tube as your mallet and a lightweight ball and an arch to put the ball through

- Playing with parachutes/fabric – you can buy specially designed play parachutes but a large, lightweight sheet or piece of fabric works just as well. You'll probably need a few pairs of hands for this so it's a good activity to play with other parents when you get together with your kids. Lift the fabric high in the air and let your children run underneath
- Treasure hunt – there are many variations on this game but for a toddler a great idea is to come up with a simple list of things to find when you go for a walk
- Running after the dog (borrow one if you don't have one!) – if you don't have a dog then running after a ball or balloon is just as good
- Kids' exercise DVD – there is a plethora of kids' exercise DVDs on the market, from yoga to Tae Bo. My kids love copying me when I do Zumba! You can also find free videos on YouTube.

PLAY: WHAT TO THINK ABOUT

11. Your own backyard
Don't forget what you have on your own doorstep. Your back yard, or any immediate outdoor space, gives your child the opportunity to explore and play in the fresh air. Always remember to check the space is safe, secure and that they are supervised.

Idea: *"Crawling games. Get down on your hands and knees, get set and go! Who can get across the room first?"* **Charlotte, mother to Eowyn, 1**

12. Active play can be about more than movement
Play doesn't always have to be about hurtling around the garden or park. This can be especially important if you have or care for a child with special needs. Keeping kids healthy is also about appealing to their brain.

Idea: *"Sensory play e.g. chasing bubbles."* *Search out different materials that can be used in an active way, from pouring water high from a watering can to chasing ribbons around a garden.* Julie, mother to Thom, 10 and Sullivan, 18 months

13. Organizing play zones
Spread different games out across rooms and areas in your home so your child has to explore and move to play. For example, set up a thimble hunt in their bedroom and balancing area (such as beanbags) in the garden.

Idea: *Treasure hunts can be indoors or outdoors. For younger toddlers, make it one familiar item to find; for older toddlers, give them picture clues to the next stage. This is a great activity for siblings to work on together.*

14. Decluttering to make games easier

Kids need room to play and that's a great reason to create as much space as you can in your home by having a good decluttering session. Get rid of old toys that are broken or not age appropriate and store away anything you don't currently use.

Idea: *"Cushions on the floor (islands to avoid crocodiles), he loves it!" And once you've played you can make a full game out of tidying everything away.* Sara, mother to **Jessica, 5 and Isaac, 20 months**

15. How much to do in a day

The recommendation is that toddlers get at least 60 minutes of physical activity per day. That doesn't need to be in one block but there's no reason to stop children being active unless they have a health condition where they need to consider how tired they get. You might find if you have had a very active day that your child wants to be less active the next day so a healthy activity in this instance might be a walk to the park or something gentle like going on the swings.

Idea: *"We love to get out into the garden as often as possible. There are so many things to do there: role play (often shopping where my daughter drives off in her car), playing in the tent, gardening or playing on the many toys." Remember, you can focus on one play area in a day if there is plenty to keep a child active and occupied.* **Claire, mother to Imogen, 7, Matilda, 5 and Cecilie, 2**

16. What to do if you don't have space

Lots of parents I spoke to when writing this book said they felt that they didn't have enough space at home to be as active as they wanted. One thing to consider is getting out of the house and searching for local low cost groups and activities (more ideas in Chapter 4). It's worth remembering that being active isn't just about running around, it's about stretching and developing strength, and finding other ways to be healthy.

Idea: *Could you find other ways to encourage healthy activities? Plant seeds and herbs to grow in pots? Make fruit kebabs? Cook healthy recipes?*

17. Bedrooms

Bedrooms can be great places for building dens and exploring. Imagine what you could find in a world under that duvet!

Idea: *"Homemade dice, one has a number and the second has an activity e.g. jumping jacks. Megan loves this and Logan loves copying her."* **Lindsay, mother to Megan, 4 and Logan, 18 months**

18. Party games
Borrow active ideas from childhood parties – from musical chairs or musical statues, to pass the balloon and bottom shuffle races.

Idea: *Try apple bobbing. Float a few apples in a tub or pan of water and then ask each child to try and catch an apple using their teeth. No hands allowed! Smaller mouths may need little apples (or you can make it really simple with grapes on a plate).*

19. Think big
If you are lucky enough to have the space and the budget then invest in a few extra bits to increase your play opportunities – a play tent, ball pool, tunnels to crawl through, or large scale outdoor games such as a kit for making giant bubbles.

Idea: *Could you make your own giant bubble kit? You'll find more information in the resources section at the back of this book.*

20. Beg, borrow, free
If the budget is a bit tight or you just want to keep spending to a minimum then many local libraries have toys you can borrow for a week or two which is a great way to keep your toddler from getting bored. For ride-on toys and bigger play equipment, check local secondhand shops, local recycling or sharing groups such as freecycle, or ebay (do check any secondhand equipment carefully before your toddler uses it). Also ask friends if they have anything stashed in the back of sheds or garages.

Idea: *"Freeze! Whether it's on the trampoline, in the garden or in the house we dance, jump or run until once of use says 'freeze.'"* **Ellie, mother to Kayla, 3**

3

PLAYING OUT

PLAY TRENDS FOR THIS YEAR: Each year, Campaign for a Commercial-Free Childhood runs National Screen Free Week to encourage children and their families to switch off media and indulge in some daydreaming and play in the great outdoors.

QUICK GAME IDEAS:

- What time is it Mr Wolf? – how many steps can you take before Mr. Wolf calls dinner time and tries to eat you?
- Hide and seek – the most mentioned activity when I asked parents for game ideas. It can be played indoors or out. Choose one child to be the seeker and everyone else has to hide.
- Sack race – set up a track in the garden and then find some old pillowcases and get leaping – who will win?
- Climbing trees (supervised, of course) – a great challenge for little arms and legs
- Gardening – if you enjoy planting and weeding then why not get your toddler involved? Set them digging or popping seeds into pots; they'll love seeing the results as everything starts to grow
- Chasing bubbles – there's something magical about bubbles, from tiny ones from jars to giant bubble kits and machines, you can keep your toddler occupied for hours

- Creating worlds with cardboard boxes – let your toddler's imagination go wild with empty cardboard boxes – what will they create? A castle? A car?
- Playing with water – try filling a large plastic container and throwing in a few toys such as a watering can. Encourage your toddler to lift their arms high and drop things into the water. What will sink? What will float?
- Bean bag balancing – a school playtime favorite. How long can you balance a bean bag on your head? Can you balance it while standing on one leg?

PLAY: WHAT TO THINK ABOUT

21. Happiness = time outside

Happiness levels are closely linked to how much time children spend outside. If we get scientific for a moment, it's to do with how much light we get to stimulate brain chemicals that improve mood and levels of motivation. Studies also indicate that children who play outside are less stressed.

Idea: *"Charlie loves climbing on anything so I leave him to it and just supervise/encourage/teach safe climbing. Gardening, I get him filling little pots with soil while I do my bits."* **Louise, mother to Charlie, 20 months and Ruby, 3 months**

22. In town

Walking around a town center might not sound like much fun but think about it from a toddler's point of view – lots of bright, colorful things to look at. It's a great (but still active) way to look at colors, letters and shapes as you walk. Also think about other things in town that will fascinate your toddler. A walk to a fire station? How about walking up and down escalators or balancing on low walls as you walk (holding onto a grown up's hand, of course)?

Idea: *Draw arrows on cards (left, right, forward, backward). When you reach a junction of a road ask your toddler to choose a card to decide which direction you will go. As you go along you can try spotting different things (number of red cars) or guess what might be round the next corner.*

23. Parks

Parks are the perfect playground for toddlers, whether you have just a local patch of grass or rolling acres of field. Almost 70% of the mothers we asked in the MumPanel survey said it was their favorite place to be active with their toddler.

It's worth asking local mothers where they take their children because the best parks are often only found by word of mouth. Many cities and towns and local governments list parks on their websites. Some green spaces are more toddler friendly than others – look for enclosed play areas where dogs aren't allowed, and some sort of toilet/changing facilities. It's always worth finding those special parks that have something extra to offer such as a maze, activity center or climbing frames. But don't just think local parks, There are also national parks to consider.

In the USA there are 59 National Parks and in the UK there are 15. Plus there are many more nature reserves that are great for wildlife spotting and big adventures! Many have their own websites and information where you can find a host of information on family friendly areas to visit with activities that are suitable for younger children.

Idea: *"Duck, duck goose" is perfect for a group of preschoolers if you meet up with other parents or carers. Get all the children sitting in a circle facing each other. One child is the fox and has to walk around the outside tapping each child on the head saying "duck." At some point they choose one child to be the goose, and to demonstrate this they tap them on the head and shout "goose!" The goose has to stand up and chase the fox, trying to tag them; the fox has to try and get back around the circle to where the goose was sitting. If the fox wins then the goose is the new fox, picking someone to be the goose. This game can keep going as long as the children are still interested.*

24. Green spaces

As well as parks there are green spaces in almost every city and town. In the UK, The National Trust owns green spaces (often with stately homes) where you can explore castles, spot red squirrels and walk alongside tame deer. It's worth checking out Get Outdoors USA for some ideas for new places to visit www.getoutdoorsusa.org/kids_corner and English Heritage in the UK www.english-heritage.org.uk/about/contact-us/enquiries/heritage-organisations.

Idea: *Shadows. You'll need a sunny day for this one! Get some chalk pieces and go outside. Encourage your child to make different shapes with their body and trace their shadow on the pavement or sidewalk. Get a large roll of paper and trace the outline of their body onto the sheet. Then you both can paint the outline together.*

25. Beaches

You might be lucky enough to have a beach on your doorstep, but even if you don't, it's worth taking a day trip to the ocean or river for the all the active things you can do with your toddler. From building sand castles on the beach, to digging moats and running down the pier – you can spend hours in the fresh air. Don't forget hats and sunscreen in the summer or protection from the wind in colder months. If it's a nippy day then collect stones, shells and pebbles to make pictures with. If you want to have a dip in the sea then it's worth checking out the water quality before you visit. You can find more information on this in the resources section of this book.

Idea: *Blow the ball! You'll need some ping pong balls and a spade. Dig a channel of the same length for each player into the sand. Then all you do is drop your ping pong ball into the channel and start blowing. The winner is the person who gets it to the end first.*

26. Leisure or recreation centers
In most towns you can find a leisure or recreation center offering affordable access to different sports including swimming, gymnastics and team games such as football. There are often groups aimed at encouraging toddlers to be active and many offer free trial sessions, so it's a great way for your toddler to try out different activities. Some centers offer memberships that include free sessions for children (these are also common in private gyms). Stop in or call your local center and see what they have to offer.

Idea: *"We have joined a running club where the children participate in fun races once a month, just generally being together and making fun as we go helps keep them active and healthy."* **Joanne, mother to Madeleine, 9, Eleanor, 7 and James, 5**

27. Other places to play
Think about other outdoor places you could take your toddler to play – specialized sports centers with tennis courts or horse riding centers, woods and forests, lakes where you can hire a boat, bike trails, caves, mountain trails, sand dunes, water parks, the farm, the zoo. Where would you go?

Idea: *Did you have an active hobby before you had kids? Do you care for kids and have an active hobby? Could you find a way to involve them? Maybe you loved rugby and you could start them at a toddler level class. Or if you are a runner how about starting on short, fun runs (or buy a stroller designed to run with your toddler inside)? It's a great way to show your kids that they can be a part of your active life.*

28. What to wear for outside games
No matter where you are in the world the one thing that can stop outdoor games is the weather. This is where forward planning becomes important

again (see Chapter One). If you have the right clothes and shoes then adverse weather doesn't have to stop play.

During my research, parents told me these were their essential items for winter: waterproof hat and gloves, thermal leggings and tops (this means fewer layers). Micro fleeces are great because they don't inhibit movement but keep kids warm. Think about the effect of water on clothing, so denim can be a problem because it gets heavy and cold when wet. Wellingtons/rubber boots are great if you have good thermal socks, otherwise opt for fleece-lined waterproof boots. For warmer but wet conditions, a waterproof slicker or mac can be a lifesaver, preventing a trek back to the car when your toddler falls headlong into the first puddle they encounter. And speaking of cars, always carry a spare set of clothes, wet wipes, bottle of water and small towel for cleanup.

In the summer you'll want lots of light cotton clothing that covers up as much of their body as possible but allows them to be cool. Also have high factor sunscreen and sun hat on hand. Sunglasses can be handy but in my experience be prepared to buy multiple pairs as they get sat on, lost and chewed!

Idea: *When winter rolls around and the snow arrives don't hurry off indoors. Build snowmen with your toddler, make snow angels and get that sled out. Wrap up warm and don't let the cold put you off being active.*

29. What to do when it rains
If the weather completely defeats you but you want to get out of the house then all is not lost. There are lots of places now that cater specifically for active toddlers. Good places to look are your local museum, local children's center and libraries. Large shopping centers or indoor malls can be handy places to while away a few hours and many have play areas and hold toddler-focused events.

Idea: *"Pirate treasure hunting – we drew a map with a big X where the treasure is hidden and went on an imaginary treasure hunt: rowing the boat, running through the jungle, digging for the treasure etc. Surprisingly active!"* **Jessica, mother to Euan, 3 and Elliott, 1**

30. No organization required
Play doesn't always have to be structured; just running around outside and exploring is fine. This kind of free play allows your child to use their own imagination and develop their independence.

Idea: *"Every day she goes into the garden for an hour, rain or shine to get fresh air and to have a run around."* **Debra, mother to Libby, 3**

4

CLUBS AND ORGANIZATIONS

> **PLAY TRENDS FOR THIS YEAR:** This year the National Trust in the UK launched their scheme "50 things to do before you are 11 ¾," and the National Park Service in the USA has "35 Parks for Play," both of which focus on getting children back to exploring the great outdoors. What could you do with your child in the great outdoors?

QUICK GAME IDEAS:

- What does that cloud look like? Take a walk in the great outdoors and then do a bit of cloud spotting – what shapes can your toddler see in the clouds?
- Frisbee – perfect for playing at the beach or in a field
- Ring a ring o' roses – sing along with actions to "Ring a ring o' roses, a pocket full of posies, atishoo, atishoo, we all fall down"
- Jumping in puddles (especially muddy ones!) – find some big puddles to jump up and down in (wellington rubber boots will be a good idea)
- Slalom race – set up some cones (large plastic milk containers work just as well) and get the kids to race around them, working on not knocking them down
- Running away from the waves at the beach – don't let the water catch you!
- Rolling down hills – always check grassy areas are free of anything dangerous such as dog waste, and then roll away

- Hula hoops – available in all sizes from baby to adult
- Kid-style basketball (ball and pot in the garden) – start at an achievable level with a large pot and work your way up to All-Stars!
- Dancing to music – turn the stereo up loud and get grooving

IN THIS CHAPTER WE'VE INCLUDED GENERAL PLAY IDEAS THAT YOU MIGHT SUGGEST OR USE WITH PLAYGROUPS OR AT HOME.

31. Take your toddler to a group

Getting out the house and taking your toddler to an organized group is good for your child and good for you. It gives them an opportunity to be active and offers chance for you to socialize and have some adult conversation.

Mothers had lots of different ideas for groups and activities to take toddlers to – some locally organized, some nationwide groups with local meetings, and something to suit just about every budget. The top three active groups suggested by mothers are swimming classes, playgroups, and active play groups for toddlers, often with soft play equipment (think Tumble Tots or Mommy and Me). You can usually find details of groups advertised in local magazines, on parenting forums, posted in stores or at the library, and through information handed out at preschool or daycare. If you are new to the world of toddler groups, then here is a quick list of what might be out there in your local area:

- Jo Jingles
- Sing and sign
- Baby Ballet
- Baby Sensory
- Church hall/Local playgroups
- Gymnastics
- Surestart groups
- Street dance
- Stageschool
- Rhythmicality
- Funfit
- Rhythm Time
- Toddler yoga
- Baby Dance
- Jumble Bees
- Jumping Beans
- Movin' Monkeyez
- Jiggly Wrigglers

- Gymboree
- Boogie Beat
- Preschool football/rugby
- Karate/martial arts

Idea: *Balloon fun. Blow up some balloons and play catch with your toddler. You can also create static by rubbing a balloon on your sweater and sticking it to the wall (or making your toddler's hair stand on end!). These are great, affordable activities for toddler groups. Do make sure you throw away any burst balloons because they are a choking hazard.*

32. Why sign them up to classes?

Some parents would like to sign their child up for a class where they are on their own (either you leave them or are in a room close by) but worry how their child will cope. I can't lie – it depends on your child. I have one who can't get away from me fast enough to get into the dance school and one who will probably cling on to me until she is a teenager. Although I don't think it's a great idea to force kids to do something they don't want to do I can see the benefits:

- ☐ It can occupy kids who are energetic and direct that energy into a useful activity
- ☐ It gives you some time alone
- ☐ It can help your child's confidence as they uncover their talents
- ☐ It can help your child make friends

Try listening to what you child wants to do but don't be disappointed if they don't like it. Children often return to an activity when they are older.

Idea: *Hotter/colder. This is a variation on a treasure hunt. Hide an item in the house (you could also play this in the garden or at a playgroup) and then ask your child to find it. Shout colder if they move away from it and hotter as they get closer. The closer they get the louder and faster you shout hotter until they find the item.*

33. Local clubs

There are lots of baby and toddler meet ups in church halls, children's centers and other local meeting places. Most offer semi-structured play for the children (plus juice and a treat) and a cup of tea or coffee for parents. It's a good way to meet other local parents and carers and have a bit of a rest while your toddler keeps active and interacts with other children. Many of these groups are free or very low cost. You'll spot information about them on local noticeboards; sometimes your local government website may have further information.

Idea: *Step! March! Put some music on or create your own drum beat with a wooden spoon and plastic container and get marching to those sounds. Have your toddler follow you and then be the leader, introduce funny ways of walking and get them to copy you. Great for getting kids of all ages involved in an activity.*

34. Nationwide groups

There are now hundreds of nationwide toddler and baby classes that are franchised to a local leader. The prices vary tremendously but toddlers can really benefit from the structure offered by classes like this. Websites such as What's on 4 Little Ones or Playgroups USA can give you some indication of what's available in your area and many of the national websites let you enter your zip/postcode for local information.

Idea: *Skipping. A good activity for getting the heart going and improving coordination is skipping. Start with the basics and get your toddler to skip across the room without a rope. Then you can try progressing to having them step over a rope that you (and someone else) hold at each end. Then move onto jumping with two feet and eventually to their own rope.*

35. Cost

Budget is a consideration for most parents and local playgroups tend to be a little cheaper than nationwide franchised groups. Most groups allow you to have a trial session to see if you like it before you commit to paying, whereas some groups will ask you to pay in advance so you probably need to make sure you can attend each week. Depending on the class, you may also need to pay for special equipment, such as sportswear.

Idea: *Dig for treasure! This is great if you have a group of kids and a local park with a (clean) sandpit. Get out in the garden or sand pit and bury some treasures for your toddler and then send them off to hunt and dig for their prize. It's a good idea to give them a rough idea of where to dig (maybe with a photo or drawing) unless you want to fill in huge holes.*

36. Meeting up with other parents

Most of the parents in the MumPanel survey met up with other parents: 88% at the park, 49% at a local coffee shop. I met some lovely mothers at my antenatal classes who I kept in touch with for years. You can also find parents to meet up with locally through online forums such as Facebook.

Idea: *"The Hokey Cokey/Pokey." A firm family favorite and one most parents can't resist (although if you try it in a coffee shop you might get a few funny looks)! The words might vary depending on where you are in the world and your own traditions but with my kids it's:*

You put your right hand in, your right hand out, in out, in out, you shake it all about. You do the hokey cokey and you turn around, that's what it's all about. Ohhh okey cokey cokey, ohhh okey cokey cokey, ohhh okey cokey, cokey, knees bend, arms stretch, rah rah rah!

You move your body with the lyrics (so right hand in) and each time do a different part of the body (left arm, left leg etc.), usually finishing with 'put your whole self in.'"

37. Setting up your own groups

If there isn't a group offering what you want for your toddler, then why not set up your own? You can start by holding meet-ups in your own home and asking people to contribute food and drinks, meaning minimal costs for everyone. If you want the group to have an active and healthy focus, then why not choose a new venue on a weekly or monthly basis such as a local park, play center or wildlife reserve?

Idea: *"Airplanes." This one is easy, stick your arms out, make a big engine revving noise and then fly wildly round the room with your toddler.* **Great for releasing your inner child! Mandy, mother to Lewis, 2**

38. Organizations for the whole family

The easiest way to have an active and healthy toddler is by setting a good example. There are plenty of organizations you can join that will encourage you to get off the sofa and out of the house as a family – the YMCA, the National Parks, wildlife and bird watching areas and zoos, just to name a few.

Idea: *Bikes, trikes and scooters. Bikes and scooters are a fantastic way to develop strength and balance. It's also something the whole family can do together. For younger toddlers look at balance bikes and scooters with seats which then grow with your child. You can also get child seats and trailers to fit on adult bikes. Remember to get well-fitting bike helmets for you and your child – even if your child is in a trailer or on the back of your bike. Many outdoor organizations welcome bike riders on their properties (check before you go).*

39. Play centers

Most towns and cities have at least one soft play center where your toddler can burn off all their energy in an enclosed, safe space. Some are designed specifically for younger children or have designated toddler areas. There are some that feature climbing frames, bouncy areas and ball pits. The entrance fee is usually fairly low and they are a good option when the weather is bad. One word of warning: be prepared to be a bit active yourself when your toddler ends up higher than they expected and you have to climb up to rescue them!

Idea: *If you can't get to a play center then how about some pirate fun? Swashbuckling is our favorite game. Pick up cushions and chase each other until you get the chance to swipe the other with your cushion. The chasee can take refuge in certain areas, for example on a small rug. As they get older you can introduce crocodiles in to in the "water." It's amazing how tiring this game can be – and how much you laugh! This is a great activity if you have children of different ages at a playgroup.*

40. Water (something for those who don't do joining!)

There are some parents who dread the idea of clubs, organizations and joining anything. And for some, the small budget means it's not possible, so I wanted to round up the chapter with a simple, pleasurable and calming idea.

If you have a local canal, lake or reservoir it's a great place to take a toddler. You can skim stones, look for wildlife and do simple things like watching reflections. Remember always to watch your toddler closely around any water and in the summer make sure you wear insect repellent. If you love nature then try short nature trails, write down a few things that your toddler is likely to find on a walk (ants, bees, trees) and get them to spot these as you walk along.

Idea: *Poohsticks. This is a childhood favorite of mine from my favorite Winnie the Pooh story. You'll need a bridge with moving water under it and a stick each. The idea is to throw your stick into the water (so it is pushed under the bridge by the current), then you run to the other side of the bridge and wait for your stick to appear and the winner is the one whose stick appears on the other side of the bridge first. Apparently, they go faster if you cheer them along!*

5

OLD AND NEW

PLAY TRENDS FOR THIS YEAR: Project Wild Thing is aimed at reconnecting 1 million children with nature, something that has been progressively lost over the last few decades. Could you meet the challenge and match your screen time with your outdoor time?

QUICK GAME IDEAS:

- Making mud pies – there's nothing better than the feeling of mud between your fingers. Just add water and you have a great pie (not to be eaten, of course!)
- Active pretend play (choose a favorite TV character who has an active job, like a firefighter) – there's no reason why role playing can't be active even if your child loves a less active character. Can you have them jump or run as that person?
- Washing the car/windows – kids love nothing better than joining in with jobs around the home, especially if it involves water and soapy bubbles
- Long walks and spotting new things – it's easy, it's free and you can do it almost any time of the year. Think about taking a camera along to capture pictures of interesting finds
- Piggybacks and wheelbarrows – a great way to get other family members involved. Set up races in the garden (piggybacks = carrying someone on your back; wheelbarrows = someone lies down, puts their hands on the floor and you lift their legs so they look like a wheelbarrow)

- Kiddie pools – fantastic summertime fun and a great place to start a water fight! You can usually buy them for an affordable price
- Skittles/bowling – you don't have to buy these pins, just fill plastic bottles with lentils or sand and then throw a ball to knock them down
- Dodge the raindrops – get your boots and waterproofs on and try skipping around those raindrops
- Singing songs with actions – toddlers love music and singing and you can make this more active by choosing songs that have actions (or making up your own). Our favorite is Incy Wincy Spider
- Pretending to be animals – pretend you are in a zoo: what noises and movements do different animals make? Slither across the floor like a snake, bounce like a kangaroo, swing your arms like an elephant's trunk

41. Encouraging your child to play

For most children their natural state is to be active, always running, jumping and skipping. But as children get older and are distracted by televisions, technology and other hobbies, how do you keep them interested in being active? How can you encourage your child to play?

Get involved yourself. I've touched on this several times in this book. The best way to show your children that being active is good is to be active yourself. And if you can find a way to be active as a family then that's even better. If, for whatever reason, you don't want to or can't actively take part then can you be involved in another way? Could you coach a sports team? Could you set up active outings with another family member?

Let your child decide. It's good to offer your child a mix of free play (their choice) and structure but try not to push them into what you think is the best choice for them or what you like to do. Just because you loved playing football when you were a kid doesn't mean your son or daughter will. Remember play is supposed to be fun!

Try things. The only way for your child to find out what they like is for them to try different activities. You might start with games, sports or activities you enjoy (or did as a child) but keep looking for new games and activities and listen to what your child has to say about each one. A child who's engaged in an activity is much more likely to continue with it in the long term.

There isn't a right way. As adults we learn that (mostly) there is a right and wrong way to do things. When children are playing this (mostly) shouldn't apply. There are circumstances where a toddler has to follow the rules (in a team sport or for a game to "work") but restrictions should be applied gently. Play at this age is all about exploration, having fun and developing, and putting too many boundaries in place could just make a child give up.

Idea: *Healthy rewards. One way to encourage your child to behave well and take part in activities is to have a reward system or chart. Often our rewards equate to something not so healthy – TV time or sweets. How about changing those rewards to something more active? A day out having fun? A trip to the park? Your child will still see the benefit.*

42. Technology and staying active
Our children are growing up in a world surrounded by technology; it's not something that they "use" but an integral part of their life. In our house the phone is my mobile/cell, the landline is the "house phone" and my children (aged 6 and 3) already think it's old fashioned and don't understand why we would have a phone plugged into a wall. My generation saw the introduction of home computers and portable phones and a pace of technological change never seen before. Our children won't see the introduction of these technologies so they aren't new or foreign to them – they are just part of their world. The temptation might be to fight against technology and drag your children away for active play. Non-screen time is vital but what if there is a way to combine active and healthy activities with tech? The internet, apps and games consoles can all be great places to find resources and instigate active play. So rather than switching everything off completely why don't you explore how you can use technology to your advantage?

Idea: *Mommy is a robot! This game always has my daughters in stitches. I pretend to be a robot (complete with silly robot voice) and I give them instructions to find my on button. As they try to find the right spot I "malfunction" and start running around the room, sticking my legs out or capturing them in my robot arms. They then have to figure out what to do to make me work (usually press my nose, kiss my cheek). It's great for close contact and identifying parts of the body.*

43. Remembering your own childhood
What were your favorite things to do as a child? What games do you remember playing with friends, siblings and family members? What clubs were you in? What sports did you enjoy? What places do you remember visiting? Our own experiences can often be the richest source of information and inspiration we have. The problem is we often forget that it's there. Take some time to sit down with a friend, partner or your child and talk about what you liked to do when you were your child's age. It can

spark long forgotten memories and enable you to connect with your child over something you once loved.

Playing with our kids is one of the most relaxing things we can do as adults; there are no boundaries (except the ones we impose) and it's an opportunity to be childlike and just let go. Remember what it felt like to run wildly down a hill, to climb a tree with no fear, to try and find a sport you loved? So put your cap on backwards, roll up your sleeves and let loose.

Idea: *Elastics/Chinese Jump Rope. This is a game I remember playing as a child. It's a great game for involving older siblings. You'll need at least three people to play and an elastic rope (you can buy these rubber bands online or in local toy stores). Two people stand about 3 feet apart with the elastic wrapped around the back of their ankles so it makes a rectangle. The third person now has to perform a set of jumps (usually to a rhyme). You can make it as complex or simple as you like but the general idea is the third person performs the jumps correctly with the elastic moving higher on each turn. If they make a mistake their turn is over.*

The jumper faces one of their friends with their left foot outside the elastic loop and right foot inside the elastic loop. Then you start jumping to the rhyme (we used to sing England, Ireland, Scotland, Wales, inside, outside, inside, on!). The first jump is so your right foot is in inside and left foot outside. Then jump and put both feet outside the elastic, then jump again and put both feet inside the elastic and finally jump up and sideways and land with your feet on top of the elastic.

44. Go retro

There are lots of play trends that come full circle, and the internet has become a place where you can research what's brand new in play but also what's back in fashion. As well as drawing on your own childhood think about a time when we had no screens at all – no computers, no televisions – what did kids do for fun then? They were active! Playing jacks, marbles and outdoor chasing games. Spend some time with your child finding out what their grandparents played at their age.

Idea: *Space Hoppers. If you are a child of the 1970s and 1980s then you'll probably remember space hoppers fondly. They are giant gym balls with ears that you hold onto for dear life and bounce your way across the playground. This year retro toys are making a real comeback so how about investing in a set of family space hoppers and having some bouncing fun in your garden or local park?*

45. Check out Pinterest and YouTube

Pinterest is a website where you can shares photos and videos in a pin board style. Most people pin images, videos and ideas around themes.

There are a growing number of boards around the theme of play and ideas for active play for children and toddlers (search for active games). It's very visual so you can see what's involved in a game or idea and it's a resource that is being constantly added to. One example is: pinterest.com/lydialoving/outdoor-and-active-play-ideas. You can also create your own boards and as you collect ideas from around the internet you can pin them to create your own catalogue of ideas. It's also worth looking at YouTube (the video website) for inspiration for active games such as song and dance games.

Idea: *Make your own pin board. Create your own boards, collecting ideas from around the internet and using Pinterest to create a personalized catalogue of ideas.*

46. Consoles

When you think of computers and games consoles, active and healthy are probably not the words that spring to mind. This isn't necessarily correct. Used in the right way, consoles can be a great active way to play, especially when the weather is bad. Focus on buying games that require your child to move and be involved, for example Wii Sports gets them up and moving, the Xbox Kinect uses the body as the controller so play always involves movement. My children particularly enjoy dancing games where they have to follow a routine or games where they pretend to be animals. Consoles are no substitute for running around in a field but they can be a handy play alternative.

Idea: *Bowling. If you've tried bowling on the console at home then why not try the real life version? Most bowling alleys cater for young children with bumpers available so balls don't roll away and ramps to help them get that strike. It's a great whole-family activity on a rainy day. It's worth checking if the alley has any special family offers.*

47. Apps

If you have a smartphone then you probably have and use apps. Maybe you use them for shopping online or playing games. Do you know there are also apps that you could use in the great outdoors? There are map apps where you can track your walks and show kids where you have been. Or healthy eating recipe apps so you can create snacks together in the kitchen. And apps you can use to identify leaves you collect on nature walks. People are developing new apps all the time and using this technology can add another layer of interest to the activities you do with your kids.

There are also accessories designed to be used with your phone and apps to play physical games such as the TheO (from physicalapps.com).

Idea: Geocaching. This is a very modern take on a treasure hunt and is suitable for the whole family. It's great for tech mad kids because you use a GPS receiver (most people use a mobile phone) to hunt for hidden containers (called geocaches or caches). There are over 2 million caches hidden all over the world and you probably have a few right on your doorstep.)

You can start on the geocaching website and look for local caches and then set off with your GPS device or phone to find the cache. Once you find the cache you write in the logbook contained within it, return it to where you found it and then share your geocaching adventures on the website.

48. Ebooks
You are reading one right now but did you know there are hundreds of children's books in electronic format? You can read together on computers, tablets and e-readers and many have interactive features. As much as I love paper books there is a world of books at your toddler's fingertips to keep their mind active and healthy.

Idea: *Lots of companies offer free children's ebooks and audio books. Try searching for "free ebooks for toddlers."*

49. Use technology to teach skills
Although we don't want to overexpose our kids to screen time it can be used in a very educational way to teach problem solving, creativity and learning through repetition (by being able to watch the same video again and again). Don't be afraid to use it as teaching tool.

Idea: *Get your child to record themselves dancing or playing a game and then watch it together. You can ask them what they like about it or what they might do differently next time. Ultimately, it's a great way to track their active childhood.*

50. And at the end of the day…creating calm time

Every toddler (and parent or carer) of that child needs quiet or wind down time. As parents we often use technology and screens to create that calm, whereas our parents would have read to us. Screen time is fine in small amounts but it's also about finding games that move your child from frantic activity to a gentler pace. These could include sleeping lions, a puzzle or card game. Or, just read a book together.

Idea: *Active reading. Choose a book where a certain word is repeated frequently (for example, We're Going on a Bear Hunt), when you say the word "bear" your toddler has to stand up or clap their hands. You can choose two or three words that are repeated and have an action for each one.*

RESOURCES

Chapter One - Active and healthy games to play with your toddler

MumPanel survey, "Playing Games with your Toddler," April 2013; 281 respondents

Physical activity guidelines for children:
www.nhs.uk/Livewell/fitness/Pages/physical-activity-guidelines-for-young-people.aspx

21 great ways grandparents can connect kids to nature:
http://www.blog.childrenandnature.org/2013/04/30/grand-ideas-21-great-ways-grandparents-and-grandfriends-can-connect-children-to-the-natural-world/

Chapter Two - Playing in

JCB Fresh Air Campaign:
www.toynews-online.biz/news/38611/Kids-spend-half-the-time-outdoors-than-parents-did

Freecycle (USA):
www.freecycle.org/group/US/
or Freecycle (UK):
uk.freecycle.org

Giant bubbles:
happyhooligans.ca/2013/03/31/homemade-giant-bubbles

Chapter Three - Playing out

National Screen Free Week:
www.screenfree.org

What Time is it Mr. Wolf Rules:
http://www.wikihow.com/Play-What's-the-Time-Mr-Wolf

Playing outside makes for happier children – multiple resources:
www.childrenandnature.org

Green Flag Award:
greenflag.keepbritaintidy.org

Water quality at beaches:
(USA) www.healthybeaches.org and (UK)
www.goodbeachguide.co.uk

Chapter Four - Clubs and organizations

50 Things to do before you are 11 ¾:
www.50things.org.uk

The National Park Foundation's Parks for Play:
www.nationalparks.org/connect/npf-kids

NCT: www.nct.org.uk

Red rover app – create meet-ups with ease:
www.coolmomtech.com/2011/10/red_rover_app_gets_even_better.php

What's on 4 Little Ones:
www.whatson4littleones.co.uk

Family Days Out (USA):
www.familydaysout.com

Chapter Five - Old and new

Project Wild Thing:
www.projectwildthing.com

Pinterest:
http://pinterest.com

YouTube:
www.youtube.com

Geocaching:
www.geocaching.com

Space hoppers:
www.space-hoppers.co.uk

Tracking walks app – Strava:
https://itunes.apple.com/ca/app/strava-run/id488914018?mt=8

Healthy eating app – HealthyU:
https://itunes.apple.com/us/app/healthyu-jr-chef/id537677869
Leafsnap: www.commonsensemedia.org/mobile-app-reviews/leafsnap

This book has been written with the help and support of MumPanel, UK-based mum marketing and insight specialists...

Sign up to MumPanel, give your opinions in surveys, focus groups and by testing products. Let brands know what mums really want with chances to win £100s of Love2shop vouchers.

www.mumpanel.co.uk

THE CENTRAL YMCA GUIDES SERIES

Happy and Healthy: A collection of trustworthy advice on health, fitness and wellbeing topics

UK
http://www.ymcaed.org.uk/hhct2

US
http://www.ymcaed.org.uk/hhct

The Scientific Approach to Exercise for Fat Loss: How to get in shape and shed unwanted fat by using healthy and scientifically proven techniques

UK
http://www.ymcaed.org.uk/sael2

US
http://www.ymcaed.org.uk/sael

The Need to Know Guide to Nutrition for Exercise: How your food and drink can help you to achieve your workout goals

UK
http://www.ymcaed.org.uk/ngne2

US
http://www.ymcaed.org.uk/ngne

The Need to Know Guide to Nutrition and Healthy Eating: The perfect starter to eating well or how to eat the right foods, stay in shape and stick to a healthy diet

UK
http://www.ymcaed.org.uk/gnhe2

US
http://www.ymcaed.org.uk/gnhe

Tri Harder - The A to Z of Triathlon for Improvers: The triathlon competitors' guide to training and improving your running, cycling and swimming times

UK
http://www.ymcaed.org.uk/thtc2

US
http://www.ymcaed.org.uk/thtc

20 Full Body Training Programmes for Exercise Lovers: An essential guide to boosting your general fitness, strength, power and endurance

UK
http://www.ymcaed.org.uk/tpel2

US
http://www.ymcaed.org.uk/tpel

Run, Jump, Climb, Crawl: The essential training guide for obstacle racing enthusiasts, or how to get fit, stay safe and prepare for the toughest mud runs on the planet

UK
http://www.ymcaed.org.uk/rjc2

US
http://www.ymcaed.org.uk/rjc

Gardening for Health: The Need to Know Guide to the Health Benefits of Horticulture

UK
http://www.ymcaed.org.uk/gfhh2

US
http://www.ymcaed.org.uk/gfhh

New Baby, New You: The Need to Know Guide to Postnatal Health and Happiness - How to return to exercise and get back in shape after giving birth

UK
http://www.ymcaed.org.uk/nbny2

US
http://www.ymcaed.org.uk/nbny

The Need to Know Guide to Life with a Toddler and a Newborn: How to prepare for and cope with the day to day challenge of raising two young children

UK
http://www.ymcaed.org.uk/ngtn2

US
http://www.ymcaed.org.uk/ngtn

50 Games for Active Toddlers: Quick everyday hints and tips to keep toddlers active, healthy and occupied

UK
http://www.ymcaed.org.uk/50uk

US
http://www.ymcaed.org.uk/50

Discover more books and ebooks of interest to you and find out about the range of work we do at the forefront of health, fitness and wellbeing.

www.ymcaed.org.uk

Printed in Great Britain
by Amazon